SON OF A LEGEND

SON OF A LEGEND

Copyright © 2021 Keith G. Pullen

All rights reserved. No part of this publication may be reproduced, distributed, or transmitted in any form or by any means, including photocopying, recording, or other electronic or mechanical methods, without the prior written permission of the publisher, except in the case of brief quotations embodied in critical reviews and certain other noncommercial uses permitted by copyright law. For permission requests contact the author via email: keithpullen2012@yahoo.com

PRINTED IN THE USA

ISBN: 978-1-7350785-4-0

Published by SBG Media Group, LLC

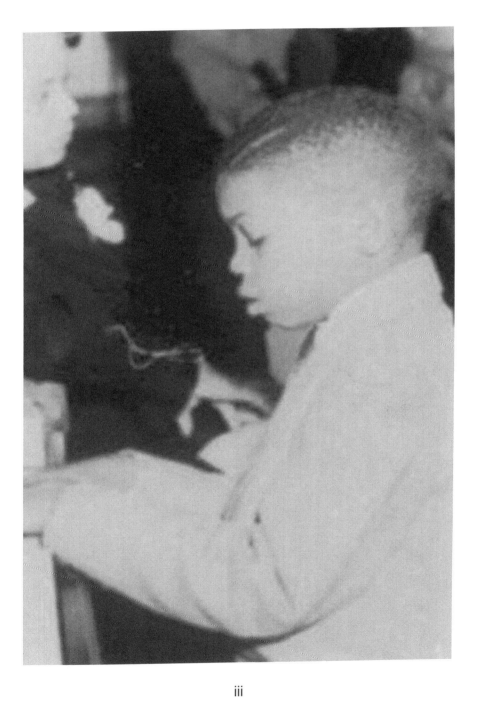

DEDICATIONS

Clifton J. Williams- My pastor, friend and most importantly brother in Christ. I want to thank you; you are the inspiration and reason to and for this book. This book would not be possible without God and you. God has used and allowed you to assist in filling the void and lack. I have had throughout my adult life in certain areas, in regard to; being a responsible adult man and most importantly God-fearing believing man in and of God and Christ in spirit and in truth. I am and will be forever grateful to who and what you are as a man, husband, father pastor, and friend. I Love You and thank God for you!

Additional thank you!

Angela Moret and Shawn Nowlin- both of you have been a huge influence on me the writing for this book. I thank you for your support, encouragement, patience, and non-wavering love you displayed towards me, during the process of writing this book. I thank God for both you and I am forever grateful for you.

FOREWARD

What do I do when the little boy whose father brought him and his sister into my office more than 30 years ago, contacts me and asked that I write the forward to a book he is writing about his father? I gladly, and humbly comply.

When Don Pullen first walked into my office in the mid- 80s, I didn't know him from "Adam", the name I gave to a poem I wrote about him and his fight for life during his latter days on this planet. Little did I know he was a famous, world renowned pianist, writer, composer, and arranger. As a matter of fact, it didn't matter who he was. He in all his fame, would be required to meet the same expectations all my clients were expected to meet. He stepped up to the challenge, saying he wanted to be as healthy as he could be, and was willing to do the work he heard I required. He told me he already knew of my reputation, and that was why he wanted to work with me; and work we did.

Throughout the years he and I worked together clinically, he struggled with the contradiction of wanting to be the best human he could be, while meeting the expectations of those he loved. In the final analysis, he opted to live his life authentically, and at the same time, protect the integrity of fatherhood, the children he had fathered, and in spite of their differences, their mothers as well.

Integrity and authenticity were two of the reasons he engaged me in his life's journey. He had ended a relationship with a woman he respected and cared for, but no longer wanted the type of relationship she wanted with him- lovers and life-partners.

He ended it, however, was angered by the fact she refused to accept the ending and respect his boundaries. He on the other hand, wanted to do all he could to make it easier for both of them. He recommended counselling to help with the transition, and said he wrote a piece in her name, (Jana's Delight), and somehow hoped that would even the score. This was the type of person Don

Pullen was, even though he was not impressed by her particular form of artistic expression.

He was sometimes more concerned about the feelings of others than he was of his own. This is one of the reasons he came into therapy with me. He wanted to be able to live his life more authentically. Don believed a lot of his childhood trauma, and the racism he experienced in the music industry and its "sliminess", was the reason for many of his problems.

We spent many hours deconstructing the things that impacted his life most. He often spoke of record companies' contractual agreements, and how many musicians and performers found themselves having to perform out of the country to a foreign market of adoring fans in order to feed themselves and their families. Many in the music industry, found it difficult to reconcile the contradictions they had to live out - their innate talent, with the limitations placed on them by their agency contracts.

Don often talked about how blessed he felt , and believed it was God's Grace that protected him from what he saw destroying so many talented musicians - mental illness, alcohol and drug addiction, and yes, domestic and intimate partner violence. He believed it was their "hidden demons", and "they should all be in therapy if for no other reason than they are Black and live in America". Don Pullen was not ordinary. He was quite extraordinary, not only as a musician, but as a (hu)man. He referred several musicians to me for mental health counselling and liked to refer to me as "therapist to the stars".

Many sessions were spent with him exploring ways to reduce stress, develop more spiritually, learn new information, and practice new and healthier behaviors. He began to meditate, change his diet, and exercise.

Then one day, he called me from Canada and told me the lump on his shoulder and chest was multiple myeloma. That was the day Don began to live with utter intentionality. He wanted to resume sessions with me so he could digest his diagnosis, talk about his life, death, and dying. He said he wanted to "tie up some loose ends" so when he died, his children would be "alright".

He created scholarships, trust funds, and formed a publishing company (AndreDon), in the name of his two oldest sons since he wasn't married to their mother. Nonetheless, Don was determined to rear all his children so they would know they were siblings. He never allowed his relationship with their mothers to interfere with the bond he tried to establish between his children. He wanted them to benefit from his life's work in equal ways, and said he made provisions for all of them in his will. Again, another example of how his role as single parent categorized him as extraordinary, as did his role as musician.

I was on vacation the day I got the call. I realized not only had I lost a friend, but the world also lost an amazing part of the human equation. But true to form, Don had honored me, in a way that was both surprising, and validating. He said I taught him the importance of active, and passive listening in order to bring about change. He wrote a song to honor my work. He named it *Listen to the* People: *Bonnie's Bossa Nova*. It was included in his 1991 release *Kele Mou Bana,* and yes Don, after all these years, I'm still listening. Thanks for reminding me to stay relevant with your artistic wizardry, and melodic instruction to always listen to the people. *Namaste.*

Elnora "Bonnie" Harrison, LMHC

Friendly Words from Dylan Locke

Keith Pullen has written a great tribute to his father, the late great Don Pullen. In my opinion Don Pullen was a true innovator within the jazz world. It was an honor to work with the Pullen family to produce a tribute concert in honor of Don Pullen and his musical legacy which was quite overlooked in his home town of Roanoke, Virginia.

In producing "Another Reason to Celebrate", a project that welcomed the modern jazz world's brightest talent to Roanoke to perform the music of Don Pullen, it was my hope to shed some light on the incredible songbook and dynamic career that Don Pullen achieved. I still feel that Roanoke has not acknowledged the incredible passion and power of Don Pullen's artistry. It was a pleasure to get to know the Pullen family and I am excited that Keith Pullen is honoring his late father in this way.

In my early conversations with Keith, I could sense the complexity of their father-son relationship; the contempt and anger created by the absence of a touring musician tugging at the adoration of a musical genius. I felt as if the concert, in a way, was a next step for Keith to embrace and accept his relationship with his father and it is wonderful to see him take yet another step towards acknowledging his father as both an incredible bright star in the jazz world and the father figure he was destined to be.

Friendly Words from Jim Shell

I first became aware of Don Pullen when I was in high school. At the time, I was avidly listening to all the jazz I could find and also reading everything I could find about it. I discovered a copy of Leroi Jones' book *Black Music* in the school library, and read in it a review of a concert Pullen and the percussionist Milford Graves had performed at Yale University in 1967. The concert was recorded and later issued as the album *Nommo,* and a couple of years after reading the review, I got a copy of the record. I had already heard the groundbreaking music of pianist Cecil Taylor, and realized immediately that he and Pullen had a lot in common; but I also realized that Pullen had a strong personal voice as well. I continued to listen to him as the records came out—the ones under his own name on the Canadian Sackville and Italian Black Saint labels, and, notably, the recordings as a member of Charles Mingus' group. A feature on Pullen appeared in *Down Beat* around this time, and I was surprised to read in it that he was from Roanoke. He had at that time received no recognition for his work in his hometown, so I had had no idea.

By this time, I had begun to write record reviews for The Roanoke Times, and one of the albums I reviewed was *Enchance,* by drummer Billy Hart, on A & M's short-lived Horizon label. Pullen was a featured performer on the record, and I mentioned in my review that he was from Roanoke. This piqued the interest of my editor at the Times, Jeff DeBell, and he interviewed Don and wrote an article about him for the paper—to my knowledge, his first bit of recognition from his hometown.

I continued to follow Pullen's career admiringly, and in the early 1990s, I found myself working with a gentleman named Bob White who was a close lifelong friend of Don's. I don't even remember how the subject came up now, but the three of us were planning to have dinner together the next time Don came into town. Unfortunately, that was around the time that Don became ill, and he never did come back to Roanoke.

That's the extent of my personal contact with Don Pullen. I'm proud that, however indirectly, I was responsible for getting him his first recognition in his hometown. As a jazz fan for some 40-plus years now, I consider him an important figure in the jazz-piano lineage—one of the few pianists (or, for that matter, musicians on any instrument) who successfully combined a more straight-ahead, conventionally tonal approach with the more daring adventures of the avant-garde. His projects combining jazz with Native-American music, as on his last album, *Sacred Common Ground,* are also notable. I hope that in the future he will continue to get the recognition he deserves, both in his hometown and all over the world.

Contents

DEDICATIONS	v
FOREWARD	vii
Friendly Words from Dylan Locke	xiii
Friendly Words from Jim Shell	xv
The Birth of a Legend	20
Stepping Out on Faith	25
Musical Success	30
Fatherhood	44
Living with a Legend	52
Spiritual Transformation	73
Cancer Strikes	86
Remission	93
The Cancer Returns	98
The Death of a Legend	105
About the Author	116

The Birth of a Legend

DECEMBER 25, 1941

On December 25, 1941, a legend was born in Roanoke, Virginia. Don Gabriel Pullen would mature and evolve into one of the greatest Jazz pianists ever. Unlike those of his era, his music stylings both impacted and changed the genre of Jazz.

Born and raised in a musical family full of singers and instrument players, Pullen was most influenced in his youth by his Jazz pianist cousin, Clyde "Fats" Wright. Classical, church, and blues music formed the foundation of Pullen's musical experiences as a youth. As a youth, Pullen played at home, local churches, and anywhere within the Roanoke community that he could.

Spirituality greatly impacted the musical gifts and talents within his family and him. Pullen's father was a preacher, and several of his aunts, cousins, and uncles served in ministry within the church.

Clyde "Fats" Wright

The church where he received his calling as a pianist was Sweet Union Baptist Church in Roanoke—one of the more popular churches in the Roanoke Valley area. Pullen's mom grew up in a strict church. When he would sing Ray Charles classic. I got a woman round and cross town. She would tell him to stop singing the devils music. She would tell him to stop singing the devils music. His mom bought him his 1st piano when he was 11yrs old. Pullen is quoted in article saying, "I often wonder if I would have been a singer if mom didn't buy me a piano."

Pullen is the fourth of five children—four boys and one girl. As a child, he was shy and bashful; however, when it was time to play the piano, he was free and at peace. Family, friends, and people within the community were amazed at his skill and gift on the piano keys. With music as his passion, his complex personality drove him to learn as much about the craft as he could. Introverted, he was not, yet he found comfort in expressing himself through art and music more than placing his focus on sports, girls, and extra-curricular activities. Pullen's musical ability with the piano garnered him a lot of attention as a youth. However, as he matured into young adulthood, he gained an affinity for the subjects of Science and Medicine. When he graduated high school, he left for college, attending Johnson C. Smith University (JCSU) in North Carolina—an HBCU (Historically Black College and University).

Pullen returned to Roanoke in 1991 for his only performance there in his musical career at the Roanoke Civic Center. This performance was a huge success was viewed and enjoyed by family, friends, and citizens within and surrounding the city of Roanoke.

Stepping Out on Faith

The year was 1960. Don Pullen—a young, aspiring Jazz pianist from Roanoke, Virginia—arrived on the campus of JCSU in Charlotte, North Carolina. Although he was granted a scholarship to study Science, less than a year later, he changed his major to Music. While on campus, he played the organ and composed and arranged music with other students. Over time, the band director and Pullen developed a musical repertoire and friendship. Confident in his musical ability, he began to perform at local jazz clubs within the Charlotte community, to include the historic Excelsior Club that was located four blocks from JCSU. The same club hosted many other jazz greats to include Nat King Cole and Louis Armstrong. During his tenure at JCSU, Pullen played at the Excelsior several times, effectively developing his experience, and creating his own niche within the genre of jazz. Pullen's exposure within the Charlotte community (and the south as a whole) quickly blossomed. Musical artists and people who followed jazz were singing his praises.

One individual who not only sung his praises but loved him was his first wife. He met her a few months into his educational venture at JCSU. There were no children from their relationship. She seemed to attract and gravitate towards successful men who were entertainers and artists. Her friends and peers were successful and famous entertainers, musicians, and artists in the Charlotte and Triad areas of North Carolinas and other prominent cities in the south. Those individuals helped influence Pullen's cache, platform, and belief in his musical career.

Conversely, his youth, inexperience, and tunnel vision focus on his career did not benefit the marriage. By the late 1960s, he was divorced, and his ex-wife went on to marry Morgan Freeman years later.

Several months before graduating JCSU, Pullen decided to leave and pursue his career in jazz music. His decision garnered mixed reviews from parents and family, but he refused to allow their thoughts and opinions to impact his choice negatively. Besides, the band director, music students, and other jazz artists within the community supported his decision.

Pullen's career as a pianist took flight in 1964 while in Chicago, Illinois. At the time, he spent a month in the "Windy City" working alongside jazz artists, honing his craft and writing music. The "Big Apple"—New York City, New York—was his next stop. Within a matter of a few months, he quickly established himself as an up-and-coming pianist. In 1966, he had his first concert at Yale University with jazz drummer/percussionist Milford Graves. Milford was known for his free-flowing, creative approach that combines art with jazz (avant-garde style music).

Not to be outdone, Pullen created his signature move of playing the piano keys with his whole forearm and hand—a tactic he perfected as his career progressed. That style did not come without its fair share of scabs, bruises, and cuts on his fingers, knuckles, and hands. Fans and other musicians have told stories of witnessing blood on the keys and his hands during live performances and practice sessions.

Despite his maturity and popularity, Pullen did not make a lot of money early in his career. By the late 1960s, he began playing the Hammond organ. The flexibility of playing both the piano and organ created more exposure for him…and opportunities to make more money. The New York club and bar scene were his meal ticket during that time, along with working with several record companies, arranging and composing music. He also started to develop positive relationships personally and musically with several jazz legends, including a few singers.

In 1971 and 1972, Pullen released commercial recordings with also saxophonist Charles Williams. He also appeared on a few of Art Blakey's tracks with the Jazz Messengers in

1972. The ability to freely compose and create his own music was critical for Pullen.

While on his musical journey, Pullen met a woman from the Bronx in 1965 who was a philanthropist, social activist, and mother. With her, he had his first child (Don Pullen, II) in 1967. Pullen adopted Don's brother, Andre, and juggled his new life as a father and aspiring jazz legend fairly well. In 1973, not only would he have another child, but he also met a drummer who connected him with a jazz bass legend who assisted in propelling Pullen's career to legendary status.

Musical Success

The bar and club scene in New York helped Pullen navigate his way through the jazz genre during the late 1960s. By the early 70s, he had rubbed elbows with several jazz greats and was the biological father of two children. He would visit his hometown of Roanoke whenever he could during his time in New York.

Although there was a considerable age gap between my mom and him, they eventually married and lived together in the Bronx, raising my sister. While waiting on his big break that would help him reach his dreams, he balanced fathering and his musical aspirations with relative ease.

The big break he was waiting for came in early 1973 when he was given the vacant piano seat within the group of legendary and renowned jazz

This is the cover art for Live at the Village Vanguard by the artist George Adams-Don Pullen Quartet. The cover art copyright is believed to belong to the label, Soul Note, or the graphic artist(s).

bassist, Charles Mingus. Mingus' group consisted of several successful musicians aspiring to solidify themselves within the jazz genre. After instant success and several quality recordings

with Mingus' group, Pullen went on to create trios and quartets with individuals from Mingus' group. The most memorable of the musicians were Dannie Richmond (drummer), George Adams (saxophonist), and Jack Walrath (trumpet). The trios and quartets started in 1979 and lasted for nine years. The George Adams/Don Pullen quartet included Cameron Brown on bass, along with Dannie Richmond.

Most of Pullen's early classics and hits were created with that quartet.

Finally, Pullen felt like he came out from under others' shadows. No longer did he have to prove himself or be compared to others. His avant-garde style of jazz was recognized and respected by his peers. The trio and quartet experiences in-studio and in public began to provide him with international and global exposure, specifically in Europe.

Although he preferred having a bassist and drummer perform with him, he accepted the challenge and opportunity to perform solo in 1975 at a concert in Toronto, Canada. His solo concert became an album deal he signed with Atlantic Records in 1972. Pullen did two recordings with Atlantic before returning to European record companies.

At the time that I was born, my dad was touring in Europe. My mother initially named me Kenneth (Kenneth Wright was a pastor at a church in Roanoke). Dad didn't like me being named after the reverend, so once he arrived home, he changed my name to Keith—a name I share with his youngest brother; who eventually lived with me, my sister and dad in Passaic NJ, during my elementary and middle school years.

Pullen loved his stardom, as did his fans in Europe, who grew to love him since he hit the scene in the 1970s. The vast majority of his music was performed there until the Adams/Pullen quartet blossomed into a success in the early 1980s. In 1986, he signed with Blue Note Records. The Blue Note label provided him with opportunities and status in the states and abroad, like no other label had. He remained with Blue Note Records until his death.

The death of Dannie Richmond began the demise of the Adams/Pullen Quartet. By that time, Pullen was an influential artist on the Blue Note label and had a bright, creative, and flexible future ahead of him. Pullen enjoyed vocal talent, he teamed up with Nina Simone and Miles Davis to produce several recordings together while working the bar and club scene. He started to write and compose a lot more of his own music as the quartet came to its end. Pullen enjoyed playing the organ in clubs and bars, although he did not have any recordings of him playing the organ during that phase of his career. His music styles ranged from blues, post-bop, and avant-garde—the latter being his favorite style of jazz and what formed his foundation for success at Blue Note.

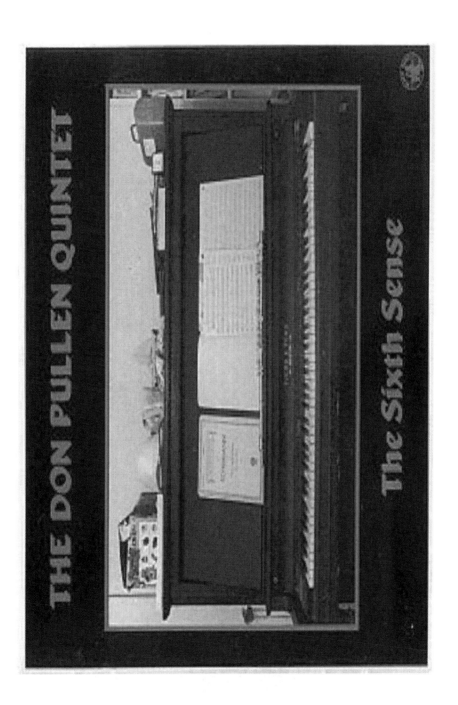

While enjoying the creative freedom and early success at Blue Note, he was also attempting to balance fatherhood and the relationships with the women in his

life.

Fatherhood

Pullen was a very complex man who loved hard and was considered a "social butterfly" by those closest to him. However, he struggled throughout his young adult life with honesty, transparency, and sharing his musical gift with, to, and for others he loved. He had to learn how to be a husband and father after I was born—both areas in which he initially struggled.

Although he was signed to Atlantic Records in 1977 and had matured into a household name for jazz in Europe, Pullen still was not recognized in the states by the majority of his peers and pundits as a star. It wasn't until the 1980s that his career truly began to mature with the formations of trios and quartets.

The ability to continue balancing co-parenting of my brothers, sister, and I, along with both women, began taking a toll on him. His goal was to attempt to keep the peace as much and as long as he could between both families.

My parents divorced in 1980. My recollection of growing up with them and my sister in the Bronx is vague. I do recall my brothers and sister not getting along well throughout their teen and adult lives, and my dad's struggles to keep the peace between them at times. The fact that my dad was consistently touring made him unavailable a lot, which impacted my siblings and me. It didn't help that he was more successful and made more money while raising my sister and me. I believe that negatively impacted our relationships with our brothers. Dad's lack of availability and the tension between my brothers and sister lasted until our father's death.

My brother, Don, died in 2006. He was in his early 40s. Don struggled the most and hardest with his personal relationship with our father, as well as balancing his feelings and experiences he had

with him versus what he saw or felt about the relationship my sister and I had with our dad. I do remember a few fun and happy times that we spent together as siblings, though. Most of the time we spent together was after my parents' divorce. My sister shouldered a lot of the "mom duties" for me at a very young age, due to our dad's tour schedule and our mom working to care for both of us. My sister's role in my life (specifically as a mom figure) was exacerbated after 1983.

Our lives were changed forever in March of 1983 when we learned my mom was sentenced to 48 years in prison (she was only 29 years old at the time). My sister was nine years old, and I was five. Before my mom's trouble with the law, my dad would drive from New York to Virginia with my sister and me to visit our family. After my parents' divorce, he continued to take us to Roanoke and let us stay with the family during holidays and summer breaks while he was touring. That provided a break for my dad and enabled my sister and me to spend time getting to know our family better. The nature of my mom's crime and my dad's inability to properly care for my sister and me because of the demands of his music career led to my sister and me living with our aunt and cousins in Salem, Virginia, for a year.

My dad was hard at work in both New York and Europe before and at the time of the news about my mom's incarceration, all while making concerted efforts to restore and reconcile the relationship with the mother of his sons, as well as strengthen the relationships with his sons. While my sister and I were living with our aunt, he was trying to figure out what his next move would be concerning us. In the Fall of 1984, he was awarded full custody of my sister and me, and we relocated to Passaic, New Jersey. We lived in an apartment complex in Passaic Park—an area known to house the successful and wealthier individuals and families within Passaic. My mother was a little over a year into her sentence at the time my dad gained custody of us (her sentence was also reduced from 48 to 12 years). Our father was at the height of his career with the trios and quartet when he obtained custody of us, which made it difficult for him. However, he was up to the challenge, and with the help, love, and support of family and close friends, he successfully raised us both through high school and on our way to college.

My brothers exposed me to the Bronx, NY community street life, their adult friends, and sports. We played basketball a lot together, and went to baseball games at Yankee Stadium which was within walking distance from my stepmom's apartment. Although, inappropriate and unsafe at times. The times and experiences spent with my brothers, where new, different, and exciting to and for me. The experiences exposed me to a life, I had not experience at home in Passaic.

Me (Keith) and The Granddaughter of a legend (my child)

Living with a Legend

Growing up in Passaic was an interesting experience. My sister and I attended the same middle and high school, both within walking distance of our apartment complex. The city was multicultural and exposed me early on to what some view as an upper-class lifestyle. I had a white, Indian, and black friend who I played with (individually and, at times, together)—all who lived within two city blocks from our complex.

By early 1985, the George Adams/Don Pullen quartet had established itself as a unique jazz group, touring throughout Europe and performing at various bars and clubs within New York City and other major U.S. cities. Work increased at a rapid pace for my dad, and he could no longer depend on the care-giving system he had set up for my sister and me. Eventually, he hired a live-in caregiver/sitter for us. The sitter was from the Caribbean and had a daughter around my age at the time. I recall the sitter having a funny accent and huge breasts. She was also very dark-skinned and had a Jheri Curl hairstyle. Her daughter and I played together at times; however, she preferred hanging out with my sister more.

My sister and I did not adjust well to taking directives and instructions from someone else in our home. Eventually, I humbled myself and began to display respectful, disciplined behavior. Conversely, my sister and the sitter never got along well because my sister just wanted our dad in the home more.

My sister and I loved to watch wrestling and play-wrestle, mimicking the wrestlers' moves in our childlike way. Snack time was also something we enjoyed together. She was not a tomboy; however, she did, at times, enjoy playing with my toys and sports games with my friends. Our age difference—as well as the fact that my sister was responsible for me in ways that a mom should be—negatively impacted our childhood relationship. She loved hard, especially when it came to me. She was very protective to the point that some would say almost to a fault.

I remember coming home from school crying and venting to her about how I was struggling with schoolwork and my peers bullying and picking on me. One particular boy in our building who was bigger and older than my sister and me used to tease, punk, and bully me. When my sister found out he disrespected me, she beat him like man...and I never had another issue with him.

She and I also struggled to connect spiritually. Although she was older, she maintained the same very independent, self-motivated attitude that she had at a young age. I believe that caused her to interact and respond to my dad's career and lifestyle choices negatively or disrespectfully at times. I didn't understand at the time because I was young, but I suppose that is why she would speak or respond to our day the way she did (that didn't stop me from recognizing when she was wrong). It's not that she was verbally or physically aggressive towards my dad. Instead, I felt as if she didn't appreciate or understand all that our dad's career and lifestyle commanded of him. Her need to want him home and all to herself caused her to act out.

The signing with Blue Note in 1986 meant not only more money but also more work for my dad. He also continued balancing his work with co-parenting my brothers in New York. My sister and I visited my brothers and their mom from time to time during our childhood. We would stay with them during the weekends and when we had extended breaks from school. My brothers' uncles and grandma lived in the same building as them, and my sister and I would hang out and spend time with them as well. My sister did not get along well with our stepmom, so as we grew older, her relationships with our brothers suffered.

I enjoyed my time in New York with my brothers and their family. I recall my sister and I being in NY with our dad's friend. She had access to the studio and site near the harbor in Manhattan were scenes from the movie Preachers Wife was being filmed. Big Alice a song my dad titled to and for an imaginary friend, was one of his greatest classic hits. Big Alice is on the musical sore and credits for the Preachers Wife. My dad's friend established relationships with popular and famous actors and Hollywood stars like Jack Nicholson and Penny Marshall to name a few. Due, to her travelling and professional masseuse career. My sister and I were able to meet some of the staff and actors in the movie like, Courtney B Vance. We were hoping to meet Denzel and Whitney but that did not happen. The appearance on the harbor at the studio was one of my most memorable experience in NY with my dad's friend. I didn't like was hearing and seeing the arguments and drama between my stepmom, brothers, and sister in regard to my dad and his relationship (or lack thereof) with each of them. I was timid, quiet, and reserved when I wanted to be. Drama, conflict, and threats of violence made me very uncomfortable and fearful. Our dad's work schedule and constant travel were hard at times for my sister and me to internalize and accept as our way of life.

During the summer and extended holidays, we would return to Roanoke to visit family and friends while our dad traveled. I enjoyed the rides from New Jersey to Virginia. At the time, my dad owned an old-school blue Cadillac. I remember listening to old-school soul music on those roughly eight-hour drives. We grooved to songs by Earth, Wind & Fire (EWF), The Isley Brothers, Michael Jackson, and more. EWF songs were our favorites, and we would all sing along as we were riding. The holidays were special in Roanoke, as the family gathered together and enjoyed each other, food, and had loads of fun.

The family loved it when my dad would start playing the piano. We would often sing along and make our own soulful Christmas music. They were truly happy times. I loved seeing the family together, enjoying themselves. Those times were also among the few times I would ever get to see my dad play the piano live. He didn't often practice at home in New Jersey, and when he did, he didn't like to do so around my sister and me. The few times he did allow us to watch him practice, my sister didn't seem as interested in him playing as I did. I was intrigued and wanted to learn how to play, but dad said he didn't have the time (or patience) to teach me. Eventually, my sister and I got a piano teacher. Those lessons didn't last long because the instructor hurt herself in our apartment building after just a few lessons. We never took lessons again.

As a child, I enjoyed playing sports. Bonding time with my dad was scarce. When he was home, we watched sports together. He didn't like hockey, but we would watch the other major sports. Dad and I also bonded over seafood, specifically crab nights. He would buy crabs by the bushel or pound, and he, his friends, my brothers, and uncle (who moved from Roanoke to live with us) would enjoy our seafood sessions. Dad didn't cook a lot when he was home, but when he did, he liked to make fish, eat boiled eggs with hot sauce, and chomp down on potato chips. I truly enjoyed our food moments together.

My sister and I shared a bedroom with a bunk bed during our early years in Passaic (dad's piano was in the middle of the room). As one of his album's covers, he chose a picture of him sitting in front of the piano in that room. The navigating of space and freedom within the confines of the home was interesting, to say the least. We used to store some things on the extended balcony of our apartment. In the complex, there was a pool, playground, garage, valet parking, weight, and exercise room, and 24-hour lobby security.

Although our living situation was what most considered "silver-spoonish," I struggled during my elementary years with my peers who judged me for being a "spoiled rich kid." Low self-esteem and attention-seeking behaviors were issues for me. My sister, however, was much more social, self-reliant, independent, and confident in who she was and what she wanted.

My dad hired a therapist in New York who he would most often visit independent of my sister and me. When we would go as a family, I enjoyed the visits and our therapist. Dad encouraged my sister and me to be open, share our hearts, and discuss whatever struggles we had. Although I was more open during the sessions than my sister, I believe the therapy helped us as a family.

The void of not having our mom in our lives impacted my sister and me differently. It didn't help that our dad didn't talk much about her. Years later, I learned he didn't want our mom contacting us whatsoever from prison. The few times I asked about her, he refused to share information about her. There were, however, a few times we visited her in Goochland, Virginia, where she was housed. As the years progressed, our dad came around and allowed our mom to communicate with us through letters.

My sister didn't talk much about our mom to my dad or me (at least not in my presence). The lack of our mom in our lives fueled my sister to never want to be "that type of mom, which ultimately pushed her to establish herself as a productive, positive person and citizen. Today, she is a lawyer and mother of three beautiful daughters—one who shares my birthday.

As for me, I struggled with not understanding why I was unable to communicate with our mom, outside of the few visits while she was in prison. Although I didn't understand why, unlike my sister and dad, I was much more forgiving and willing to attempt to comprehend the lifestyle choices that landed our mom in prison.

Our dad left money and whatever other necessities my sister and I needed with our sitter when he would leave for work. The longer the time away, the more he would leave. There were a few times when he was gone for four to six months or longer. When he returned—especially after a long touring stint—he would be surprised at how much I had grown.

I sometimes felt as if it was like pulling teeth to get our dad to provide money for our basic needs, specifically clothes for my growing stature. However, when I found out that several trust funds, including one for college and royalty monies, were left for my siblings and me, I understood why he didn't spoil us with his wealth. At times, he even made us work for an allowance as we grew and matured.

Dad nicknamed me "Jake Bone" and "Jake." He would say, "Jake! My God! How much more are you going to grow, and when will it stop?!" He composed a song after my nickname called "Double Arc Jake." He also had a song he dedicated to everyone else close to him, including my mom, sister, brothers, his female friend, a male friend, and a few musicians from his trios and quartets. The song had a spiritual and personal connotation and meaning, to and for my dad, as did all the songs he wrote and dedicated to his friends, family and loved ones, which included songs for my mom, ,siblings and a few musicians he played with. Dad felt like at times, I displayed a split personality and struggled to maintain consistent behaviors, which established the genesis to and for the title of the song.

Dad often brought back with him mementos, money from other countries in bills and coins, photos, clothes, and various other items when he returned from his tours. The most memorable surprise was an autographed picture of him with Bill Cosby. The Cosby Show was a favorite of my sister and me, so to see our dad with Mr. Cosby was truly remarkable!

When he wasn't touring, dad had gigs and performances at historic nightclubs in New York. I saw him perform live twice. The first time was at a club in New York when he performed a song that was and still is very emotional for me to listen to.

I recall crying in his arms on stage at the piano after he performed. He dedicated the song to a close friend of his who had died. The other time was when he was live in concert in North Carolina. I was a young teenager at the time. He allowed my sister, certain family members, and me to travel with him. It was an awesome, memorable experience—and my first at a coliseum.

The most memorable experience I have is from when he took my sister and me to San Juan, Puerto Rico for a vacation (we were both young teens). That experience was and remains the only time I've flown on a plane. Although I got sick in the air on the way there and back, the time spent in San Juan was once in a lifetime. The majority of our dad's touring was done in Europe and Puerto Rico, where the fans and his peers loved him. The beach waters and scenery were like nothing I had seen before. Dad allowed my sister and me to choose items to bring back home as souvenirs of our time there. I am still grateful to this day for the experiences (although not many) when I traveled and saw my dad doing what he loved.

Dad was not a huge disciplinarian. There were, however, a few times when I blatantly disobeyed him as a young boy and was disciplined accordingly. One time, he slapped me so hard, I flew across the room into a wall. Another time, I was consistently late on my curfew, and I ran through the apartment with a piece of Styrofoam in my pants that covered my butt to avoid the sting of the belt.

My sister and I had our moments when we argued, but we never got into a physical fight. I was fearful of her, especially when she became aggressive in any way. Plus, I never liked the idea of fighting anyone. During my elementary and middle school years, I didn't have what I now know to be "real friends"; I had peers I associated with. I did, however, develop friendships with two guys who lived in downtown Passaic. I am still good friends with one of them today. He became like another son to my dad, and we spent a lot of time at each other's house from 6th grade all the way until we graduated high school together. We had our ups and downs, from working our first job together at Giants Stadium in East Rutherford, New Jersey, to him and another "friend" attempting to fight me one day while walking home from school.

To my surprise, my dad knew about me being bullied and teased by my peers. He even knew the friends I worked with were bullying me. One day, he pulled up in his car as my friends and I were walking home. At the time, they were threatening me, throwing rocks at me, and saying disrespectful things about my family. When my dad pulled up, he got out of his car and started screaming and chasing my friends as they ran away. After that incident, the friendship with the friend who spent a lot of time at our house during the early years suffered. Plus, it took a while for my dad to forgive him, and my dad forbade him to come into our home.

I had another friend who lived near me in Passaic Park. Although he was Indian, he and I were close. He was the only other friend my dad allowed to spend time in our home. On the nights when he would stay over, my dad would stay up late and watch sports with us. One memorable time was the night one of the biggest upsets in boxing history occurred: Buster Douglass beat Mike Tyson. My friend was rooting for Buster to win, but my dad and I thought he was crazy! Buster didn't stand a chance against "Iron Mike"! Well, we were wrong about that one!

My dad rarely displayed a strong, masculine personality. He did not train or teach me to fight; neither did he steer me towards sports or any other activities that required physical contact. However, dad never allowed me to be taken advantage of or mistreated in his presence. When he came home and learned about such incidents, he dealt with it and any individuals involved swiftly. He was like that with everyone he loved, especially his children.

I remember not knowing how to swim, so my dad signed me up for lessons. A local guy that swam a lot at our pool and who used to be a lifeguard was the one who taught me. One day, while dad was home, he came down to the pool in a leather outfit (I used to call it his "Eddie Murphy: Raw Outfit"). In my excitement, I decided to show off and jumped into the deep end—the 7' – 9' section. I began drowning and screaming for help. The lifeguard was totally unaware, so my dad (who was closest to me) jumped in and saved me. Thinking about dad's "Eddie Murphy" suit getting wet is funny to think about and laugh at now, but at the time, it was no laughing matter.

By the time I entered the 7th grade, our uncle was no longer living with us. However, he and a few of my dad's close friends continued to visit and stay with us from time to time. One friend, in particular, spent more time with us than others. She impacted and eventually changed my dad's life like no one else.

She was from New York and was a professional masseuse and health/exercise freak. She loved my dad's music and supported him both personally and musically throughout his life until his death, even assigning her control over his musical affairs and estate when he died. During my middle and high school years, when she was not working and traveling, she was living with us. She encouraged and supported my sister and I a lot while exposing us to her healthy eating and positive exercise habits, including yoga. She always celebrated our birthdays and spoiled us with Christmas gifts as well, even when she was not living with us. She also took care of our personal needs and other responsibilities (i.e., doctor visits, dentist appointments, school meetings, and social community outings). Sometimes, my sister and I would get to travel with her to New York to visit her loft and hang out with her in the city while she ran her errands. My sister and I enjoyed those moments, although they were few and far between.

She was also a lover of both people and animals in need—some would say almost to a fault. She specifically loved cats and gave our family our first cat. Eventually, we had three cats living with us until one of them died. As my sister and I got older, and our dad got sick, the two remaining cats went to live with dad's friend in New York.

I thought it was strange that dad had his close male friend spend the night with us at times and, when he wasn't spending the night, his female friend (who had become like a stepmom to my sister and me) would be there. I recall walking in on my dad in bed with his male friend a few times, as well as him in bed with his female friend. I never saw him in bed with both at the same time, though. My sister also witnessed dad in bed with his male friend. She and I never really discussed it, but it made us uncomfortable, nonetheless. The freedom we once had to pop in and check on our dad to try and enjoy our intimate times with him in his room diminished.

I enjoyed sneaking and hanging out in my dad's room when he was gone. I took great pleasure in listening to his Michael Jackson and Full Force albums and would dance to them. I also rummaged through his bills, coins, clothes, and other items from foreign countries. Doing those things always excited me, as well as when I relaxed in his king-size bed and watched movies, VHS tapes of recorded award shows, and sitcoms.

My sister would sometimes join me, mainly when I watched the award shows and sitcoms.

The intimate times my dad and I spent together in his room watching sports, TV shows, and talking was all but over once his friends began to spend the night and live with us consistently. I was troubled by the change but didn't know how to approach my dad about it. As a result, those illicit adult behaviors continued for several years.

I remember struggling with Math during middle school—a struggle that landed me in night school in order to graduate from high school. While I was battling my way through, my sister was finishing up high school strong as the Class President, a cheerleader, track runner, prom queen, flute player, and drama queen of plays. It seemed as if there were nothing she could not do! The precedent she set for me as I headed into the same high school was like no other.

During my 7th-grade Math struggles, my dad's female friend spent an entire weekend teaching me multiplication. She was determined, too! She would not let me go outside until I learned my multiplication tables from 1 to 12. To this day, I know my times tables and can answer any one of them in less than three seconds. I saw her recently, and we laughed and joked about that time in my life.

Although my dad couldn't be there physically for parent-teacher conferences and school activities, he did interact and communicate with my school and teachers. I still have some of the letters my dad wrote to my teachers in middle school and throughout high school, as well as the teachers' responses. At the time, I had no idea he was doing those things. It wasn't until after his death that the letters were discovered.

Spiritual Transformation

The same weekend my dad's friend had me in the house learning my multiplication tables, my dad came home and told my sister and me he needed to talk with us (my dad's friend wasn't there at the time). I remember the moment vividly.

During this time, I had begun to come out of my shell and socialized a lot more with neighborhood friends. However, I was still being bullied and taken advantage of by my classmates and friends. Although I was excited about finally learning my times tables, I was still in my feelings about not being about to go outside to play. My emotions were made worse because I could see my friends outside playing basketball in the driveway directly across the street.

That weekend was one of the most agonizing ones of my young life, especially after hearing the news my dad dropped on my sister and me.

I was sitting in the living room, and my dad called for my sister to join us. He sat down and boldly told us that he felt convicted about knowing that my sister and I have seen him in bed with his male and female friends. He then proceeded to tell us that he was gay and that his male friend was his lover.

I received his confession and attempted to understand his lifestyle choice. I know it was not easy for him to tell us. The same could not be said for my sister. She cried, became very emotional, and bombarded my dad with questions about how and why he chose to live that way. I believe that with my sister being older and understanding more about the gay lifestyle than me at the time, it contributed to her reactions and responses to and from my dad. However, my dad did not receive her reaction well. I believe it negatively impacted their relationship from that point forward, specifically regarding the trust and ability to confide in one another.

The intimate bedroom relations with my dad, his gay lover, and his female friend continued until his gay lover died in the early 1990s. The rumor was that he died from complications associated with AIDS.

During the '90s, my dad began to embark on a transition with his music style and genre. The change not only impacted his music and legacy like never before, but it also (in my opinion) contributed to his eventual death from lymphoma cancer.

Pullen was a free spirit, and although his personality was complicated at times, he never lacked the faith to try new and differing things in music that most would not even consider or understand. His desire to push the envelope with his musical gifts, creativity, and desire to include people of different cultures, backgrounds, and musical art talents gave birth to the African Brazilian Connection ("ABC"). The group consisted of a bass player from Brazil, a saxophonist from Panama, a windpipes/chimes artist from Senegal, West Africa, and a drummer from New York. (The gentleman from Africa is the father of the well-known musical artist, Akon.) The group was very successful, with their second album rising to the fifth on the U.S. Billboard Top Jazz Album chart. Up to that point, jazz had not seen such an ensemble of different instruments, cultures, and musical gifts on display—nor were they ready for how ABC would impact the genre as a whole. ABC was Pullen's last group, producing three albums—one recorded live—before his death.

As I was completing my middle school venture and preparing to attend high school, I experienced puberty at a level unlike ever before. I found myself in a state of confusion concerning some of the changes in my dad's lifestyle choices and behaviors, specifically his style of dress and overall appearance.

My sister and I noticed our dad was dressing very differently, as well as using commercial hair and skin products to help enhance his facial features, tend to the receding of his hairline, and minimize the appearance of his gray hair. It wasn't until years after his death that I learned our dad modeled throughout his career, with the vast majority of his modeling done during the late '80s and ABC years. I now realize that modeling contributed to the drastic changes he displayed.

Pullen loved dance and art, fusing them into his music. There were times when he returned home after being on the road, dressed in African and

European garments to include chains, bells, and other accessories that made unique sounds. He would jokingly dance and prance around the house, attempting to mimic African and different cultures' dances. My sister and I, family, and friends noticed drastic changes in Pullen during those years.

Eventually, he teamed with Garth Fagan—a Jamaican dance choreographer—and founded a modern dance company in New York. Garth and Pullen blended dance with music, chants, and songs from the Chief Cliff singers from India on Pullen's last album with ABC. The project with the Garth Fagan dancers and the Chief Cliff singers began in the early '90s until its culmination in 1994. Some jazz pundits and peers did not believe in or understand what he was trying to accomplish by joining art, dance, and music; neither did they think it would be as successful as it was.

When I became a man and matured spiritually, I better understood the changes my dad experienced and the personalities, behaviors, and spirits he entertained that ultimately changed his life forever. I believe some of those experiences had a negative impact on his life, with the most significant being the decline in his health and eventual death from lymphoma cancer in 1995, coupled with the complexity and intimacy of his relationship with his female friend. Although she was a great aid to the personal growth and success of my sister and me, as I got older and into my later high school years, I began to sense she had motives, objectives, and plans beyond my dad, sister, and me as a family. I believe she desired to manipulate and control not just my dad, but the legacy of his music.

Pullen's relationship with her had its ups and downs at times, even before the drastic changes to his style of music, dress, and appearance. In private, dad told me he didn't know how much longer he could or wanted to put up with her controlling, manipulative, and attention-seeking behaviors. One thing, in particular, that got on his nerves was when she would consistently leave long, drawn-out voice messages on his answering machine (I can vividly recall him playing some of the messages back for me). She would talk until the machine cut her off—and then call right back to continue her message. I also recall several times when he would come home and show me the number of voice messages she left for him...often eight or more!

That specific behavior continued throughout their relationship, only declining slightly during the years my dad was sick with cancer. However, he did rebuke her about her incessant calling and other behaviors during the early '90s when he was in the process of his face, body, dress, appearance, and spiritual transformation. I believe my dad did not want me to see or know about the discussion they had regarding their issues while I was home, but the discussion got heated. I heard him yelling, telling her he was fed up with her leaving the abundance of messages. That was one of the few times I witnessed my dad enraged with her. That night, she left our home in tears.

At times, being a masseuse was a strenuous career path for my dad's friend. In addition to the care of her clientele, she also tended to family and friends who were sick or had other personal issues that negatively impacted them. Health, fitness, dieting, exercise, and spiritual serenity built the foundation of who and what she was. Early on, she exposed my sister and me to her various foods, exercises, hygienic practices, and spiritual rituals. I also learned (after walking in on her and my dad in bed) that she exposed my dad to her lifestyle and spiritual rituals as well. I believe the culmination of years of her exposing my dad to the following were all contributing factors that led to his death from cancer:

- Massaging and rubbing his body with oils, fragrances, and lotions.

- Entertaining via the use of crystal balls, masks, idol images, and figures.

- Allowing cats to rest on her and my dad's body while they rested.

- The consumption of certain foods and drinks.

Several times during my middle school years, I vividly remember walking in on the two of them with her on top, rubbing my dad down while the cats moved around in the bed. A few times, the lights were either dimmed or out completely, and the room seemed to have a weird odor emanating from it. I also remember being in his bedroom while he was gone and seeing crystal balls, chains, beads, and other types of jewelry sitting out on his dressers and tables. There were also masks, weird-looking art pictures, paintings of figures, and images that I now know were being idolized by my dad and her. I honestly didn't know how to feel, but I knew something wasn't right. The fact that her behaviors were taking place during the years when my dad also had a gay lover in his life compounded my thoughts about what was happening to and with the drastic changes in my dad's life and his music—and proved to traumatize me at the same time.

As I got older and entered my high school years, I began to reflect on the times she would massage my sister and me. She also had us place our hands on our stomach and tell us, "The heat and energy are healing you and bringing peace to your spirit." She called that healing practice "Reiki."

My sister never talked to me much about the things we witnessed that happened between my dad and his lady friend. I spent considerably more time sneaking into our dad's room than she. After he told us about him being gay, it seemed like my sister wanted nothing more to do with sneaking in there when he wasn't home.

In young adulthood (specifically when my dad was sick with cancer), I used to reminisce about how my dad's friend would often have spiritual talks with me as a child, telling me there was something unique and special about me. She would go on to say she could "foresee" me doing great things to help people, particularly on and at a spiritual level. I also remembered how she would project her spiritual lifestyle onto my sister and me—and how she would react when I was not receptive to some of her practices and rituals. I found it odd that she would not have spiritual talks with my sister and me at the same time. I would come home or happen to catch her and my sister having mommy-daughter time, and I was left to feel as if she didn't want me in the midst. I believe that in her own way, she was grooming my sister to not focus on my dad's spiritual state but to, instead, have my sister put her faith in her as "the adult who had the best interests of my sister's spiritual being and life at heart."

Presently, my sister is much closer to my dad's friend than I am. A reason for that is because she has, through the years (and currently), lived closer to her. I have since forgiven her for the things that she did that I believe contributed to my dad's death, as well as misappropriating and mismanaging funds and resources within my dad's estate. The relationship I have with her since my dad's death has had its ups and downs. However, I believe we now have mutual love, respect, and understanding of each other and are grateful for the life, legacy, music, and love we both experienced of and from my dad.

Cancer Strikes

The changes in my dad's life—specifically spiritually—impacted not only me but everyone close to him, including my brothers and the relationship he had with them, and their mom. As best I could, I pressed my way through life, leading up to the day dad was diagnosed with lymphoma cancer in 1994. At the time, my sister was amid attempting to finish up college, and I was maturing into young adulthood quickly, continuing to grow tall like a weed. I also started night school classes for Math during my junior year in efforts to graduate on time and began my first job working at the Meadowlands in East Rutherford, New Jersey (Giants Stadium). My two best friends from middle school to high school (the ones who punked and bullied me through the years) worked with me as well. We had fun and crazy times working together, and I really enjoyed it. I have always been a huge sports fanatic and loved being able to watch the games played live in the stadium. (BONUS!)

Attempting to navigate growing into a young man without my dad in the midst consistently and knowing something was not right with him physically and spiritually was not easy. As I progressed toward the end of my junior year in high school and entered my senior year, I began staying at home by myself at times when my dad went to work for the day or on the weekends. My dad was a workaholic. Besides our trip to San Juan, Puerto Rico, when my sister and I were young, I don't recall him ever taking an extended break from work for himself or with family. I do remain grateful for the time I saw him perform live at a club in New York and again at a concert in North Carolina. Although my dad trusted me enough to stay home alone at the age of 16, I didn't totally abuse the freedom and opportunity. I did, however, attempt to drive my sister's car after taking a few driving lessons before I had my permit. That experiment turned into a disaster, as I reversed into a parked vehicle across the street from our apartment complex.

Dad was not as open about his cancer diagnosis as he was about his gay lifestyle. From the time I was young up until he could not do so anymore, he rarely played the piano in the apartment. Around the time I found out he had cancer; he began to play the piano more frequently at home. A few times, I came home to him playing or writing sheet music while seated at the table. There were visible signs that something serious was not only going on with his physical body but also him personally. He had swollen lymph nodes on his face, neck, and body, along with his sudden desire to play the piano more often in our home that was indicative of yet another change occurring. A few times, I snuck up on him while he was using facial and hair products to "mask" the impact of the cancer. It was a scary, weird feeling. Eventually, he had minor plastic surgery done to his face. He shared with my sister and me that it was partially due to health issues, but I don't recall him ever telling us it was cancer or the type of cancer he had.

From 1992 until his death in 1995, dad's physical and spiritual changes were dramatic. However, he stayed on his grind. Once he was diagnosed with cancer, his goal at all costs was to complete the project he began with the Chief Cliff Indian singers and Garth Fagan dancers. He also continued working with other notable jazz peers and artists, including the legendary Roots crew from Philadelphia, Pennsylvania, as well as reverting to doing solo and trio works.

After his initial diagnosis of cancer, the primary adjustment for me was getting used to how his face looked and continuing to see the lymph nodes swell as the disease progressed. No matter what we did, we could not stop, slow down, or deter dad as it related to his music and lifestyle. Even after the cancer went into remission and returned, his female friend finally got the revelation that dad was going to live and lead his life in and through his music as he desired. In no way was he going to let cancer, anyone, or anything else stop him. He even appeared to be more patient with others during his bout with cancer before he went into remission. Although he worked just as hard (perhaps even harder) during that time, he didn't appear to be fatigued as he should or could have been.

I do recall the time, prior to the remission of the cancer, when dad found out my brother Don (his namesake) was using drugs and wasted the money dad supplied him with to finish grad school at New York University. (My brother had two small children at the time, one which is named Don Pullen, III.) The news of my brother's drug habit greatly grieved my dad. It was one of the moments I can recall being at home and hearing my dad express his displeasure with something that had occurred. After disconnecting the call from my brother, dad shared with me what happened. Although I was confused and in my feelings about seeing my dad angry and grievous, I was also concerned for my brother.

Disappointingly, dad was not consistently in the home and in my life to teach, train, and discipline me as it related to sex, women, drugs, and future career choices. He also did not participate in activities that many fathers do with their sons, like teaching how to tie a tie and go fishing, to a ball game, etc. There were a few moments when we talked, and he would share his heart about an issue or situation he was going through, or that was impacting him in some way. I now know that not only did those moments happen for a reason, but I also believe

God allowed me (of all people) to be home at the precise times when my dad was free to share with me what was going on and how those things impacted him.

The strength and perseverance my dad had throughout his life and, more specifically, when he battled cancer was like none other. The doctors, some family, and close friends felt my dad was stubborn and prideful for continuing to put his hand to the plow and work as he did, considering his health situation. However, what would happen surprised them all, including dad.

Remission

I did not have much knowledge about the type of cancer my dad was diagnosed with. He didn't talk much to me about the specifics, and one of the few times I recall asking him a direct question about it, he skated around sharing with me its cause. I assumed (and he led me to believe) his years of alcohol abuse, smoking, and drug use early in his music career, along with the everyday stressors of life, contributed to the disease.

The adults in my dad's life and those close to him, including my aunt, uncle, and female friend, never spoke directly with or to me about the disease nor its results. I personally felt like I was old and responsible enough to know what was going on and the truth about his condition, however, it was kept from me. Although I understood why dad wouldn't talk much about it, I worried about how much longer he would live, especially after I learned how fast and aggressive cancer could spread and lead to a premature death. Amidst it all, I condition myself to believe he would live until I graduated high school, which was a year away at the time.

I don't recall precisely when his cancer went into remission. I do, however, remember my family and dad's close friends being very excited and that he seemed rejuvenated and even more focused on continuing his music and artwork. While the cancer was in remission, dad still had to keep going to his regular doctor's appointments and go through testing to ensure the cancer cells would not return.

During the last year of his life, dad and I were home a majority of the time. My sister would come home every so often from college, and dad's female friend would come by now and then to check on dad and me. I struggled with seeing him in his condition, and although the cancer was in remission, it was still difficult for me to see the condition of his face and body deteriorate due to the cancer, even after the minor facial surgery he had.

I recall becoming rebellious at that time in life. I engaged in poor behaviors (i.e., smoking, partying, and gambling). At the age of 17, I had sex for the first time in my home while my dad was gone. Throughout my teen years, many of my peers (specifically the girls) thought I was weird, introverted, and a punk. The girl I had sex with felt sorry for me and only did it out of spite to get back at a guy who knew both of us and some of my other friends. During the act, I was so nervous, thinking my dad would come home and catch us.

I soon began to feel like I could easily continue getting away with my poor behaviors, especially when my sister and dad's female friend were not in the home. I also knew that dad could not discipline me like he used to because of his health. I also believed he was much more focused on finishing his music and art project than he was on me.

I used to hang out with a crew of friends and gamble after work. Often, I came home from work with over $100.00 in tips alone. I also sold weed at the time and had it hidden under my bed. On one occasion, dad kept paging me. I knew he wasn't feeling well, so he made sure I had a page and instructed me to respond in case of an emergency or if he needed me at home immediately. Well, I continued to ignore his pages, attempting to win back the money I had lost. That day, I ended up coming home close to 11:00 p.m., tired and upset about the lost monies and the fact that I knew dad would be pissed off if he heard or saw me coming in that late. I attempted to sneak into my room quietly (I was staying in my sister's old room, which was right next to the entrance of the apartment). As soon as I stepped foot in the room, I noticed the weed I had hidden under the bed was exposed. Before I could get up off my knees, dad was standing over me. He looked hurt, disappointed in me, and was in obvious physical pain. Surprisingly, he didn't threaten to beat or punish me. Instead, he expressed his disappointment and stated he felt hurt that I would put my lifestyle choices and poor behavior before his health and being there for him when he needed me.

The initial shock of not being punished or beaten diminished after our talk. I realized I had hurt my dad like never before and that the pain he was in was severe.

The Cancer Returns

The trauma of seeing my dad in physical and emotional pain after he found my weed stash stuck with me for a while. Shortly after that incident, the family found out the cancer cells had returned (I was not told by the family or my dad about the cancer returning until months later). The disease returned with a vengeance. Not long after, my dad died.

I remember one of the last times the family got together at the house before the cancer caused my dad to go to the clinic for treatment. I can't quite place the exact time, whether it was during the initial diagnosis or once the cancer returned. I do, however, remember the gathering was special, not only because my brothers and immediate family were there (which was rare), but also because part of the reason was to celebrate my birthday and me fulfilling the night school requirements to graduate high school.

At the gathering, my sister stood in the midst of everyone there who was celebrating me, and the quality time spent with dad, and gave a speech about me. She basically spoke about how she hated me, disliked living and growing up with me in the home, and how she despised having to be like a mother-figure to and for me. She was in tears as she continued, stating she felt cheated out of the life she desired as a girl due to my dad's music career, lifestyle, mom not being in our lives, and the relationship she had with me while growing up. Needless to say, everyone in attendance was in a state of shock. No one—not even my dad—ever spoke to me personally about the events of that day. Although I have forgiven my sister, I have thought about that incident on and off for years. I believe it did not help my dad deal with trying to rectify and make peace with himself, my siblings, and me for the path he chose to walk in life.

Before his passing, dad was committed to working and finishing up his projects, including his last album. I admired the fact that he would not let the cancer returning stop him from his work commitments while trying to continue taking care of and providing for me, my siblings, and family.

When he was hospitalized and eventually went into hospice at my aunt and uncle's house in East Orange, New Jersey, I wanted to take that time to apologize and make peace with my dad over the weed incident but was unsure of how or when to do so. My brothers, other family members, and friends who had not been around as much during his initial stint with the cancer were communicating and attempting to maintain closer contact with dad that time around.

By the end of 1995, my dad's friend started the process of controlling the future of my dad's music, money, and the material things he had gained throughout his life and career. I recall her only wanting myself and other visitors to see my dad at specific times when he was in the cancer clinic in New York. I only recall being permitted to see dad twice while he was in the clinic. My sister, aunt, uncle, and a few other family members went more often than I did.

The first time I went to see him, he seemed in good spirits, although he was tired and groggy and didn't quite remember much. He spoke to me about how someone had given him a bunch of papers to sign and information to discuss, and he seemed agitated and upset about it. I could tell he was tired and not very coherent, but it was apparent he was responding to the treatment he was receiving. He didn't appear ready to die, and he definitely didn't like how the family responded and reacted as if he was going to dies soon by wanting him to sign papers and prepare for his death. Dad and I didn't talk long during that first visit, as it was difficult for me to see him in his condition.

The second time I went to see him, he was seated upright and seemed a lot more energetic and coherent. I recall my brothers and other family members helping him to shave and assist him with trying to move around, enjoying each other's company. At the time, I was still in my feelings about the incident concerning him finding my weed and other things that happened prior to the cancer returning. When I approached his bedside, I apologized and told him how much I loved him and was sorry for my bad behaviors. He accepted my apology and then began to encourage and edify me. He told me how he always loved me and knew I was a special child—his special child. He shared his heart about how he felt bad at times about not being in my life and doing things with and for me that most dads do, due to his music career. He also asked (in his own way) for my forgiveness for him not being the dad I wanted and needed him to be, and that although he did not regret the choice to choose his career over my siblings and me, he realized he could have handled some things differently concerning his time investment in us.

My dad's friend was sure to have my dad sign off on all legal and personal paperwork that allowed her to manipulate and control my dad's music, money, and material things. The majority of that was done when my dad was not coherent. She did those things when he was in no position to agree to the significance of what he signed. As well, she did not discuss her plans in detail with my siblings and me. Neither did she mention what my dad had planned, prepared, and discussed with her concerning his music, estate, and legacy. She also came back to us with reports of how our dad was doing, saying she had spent all night with him, massaging and oiling him down, praying for him, and nourishing him with certain healthy foods and juices that were supposed to fight against the cancer cells—still using a form of idolatry to manipulate my dad for her own purposes.

Before I left my dad's side that day after my second visit, he told me he believed and knew that God was with me and would remain during my life's journey. He stated he was grateful for the opportunity to make peace with me and for the apologies we both offered as we shared our hearts with each other about our relationship and my future. Although I don't remember the conversation word-for-word, the memories of that day at the clinic are still real and strong within me. That conversation gave me hope and helped me to believe that dad would, indeed, pull through to be alive for my graduation.

The Death of a Legend

APRIL 22, 1995

The relationship between my dad and uncle strengthened during the later years of dad's life, and I was pleased to enjoy some of their special moments together. A year before my dad's passing, a birthday celebration was held at my uncle's house. The family was unable to celebrate dad's 50th birthday due to his busy schedule and the cancer striking his body (he was experiencing health issues at the time and unable to celebrate as he may have liked). However, as a family, we had a great time and made up a song that my uncle sang during the celebration. Although my dad was turning 53, the chorus of the song was, "Ain't nothing wrong with 50; it's just half of a 100!" That is a moment I have thought about through the years and still do when the family is together, especially at my uncle's house.

The last conversation I had with my dad at the cancer center not only gave me hope for his future, but it also gave me peace concerning his life and our relationship. After that day, I felt totally different than ever before about his life, music, and our relationship. I was encouraged that regardless of what happened with my dad's future, God was in control. Dad was at peace and wanted the rest of the family to be as well. Much to my disappointment, some members of the family—specifically my sister—did not seem to harness the same level of peace that I had as dad transitioned from the hospital to hospice care.

In March 1995, dad completed his final musical recording with the Chief Cliff Indian singers. A premiere for the album was scheduled for later that Spring. However, he had worked to prepare his protégé to perform his music…just in case. His protégé eventually performed dad's songs live at the premiere for his final album titled "Sacred Common Ground." Pullen's protégé went on to compose and record his own music. He produced 12 jazz CDs, won an Emmy Award in 2016, is currently the Director of the Global Jazz Master's Program at Brooklyn College, and teaches Media Scoring. I recall my dad tutoring him at our apartment in New Jersey and was able to see him perform my dad's music. I did not spend a lot of time around him, but I recall him being a humble man who was honored to not only learn from my dad but also to have the opportunity to play his music.

When dad made in public that he would not perform the final album's premiere and that he handed the reins to his protégé, it was then that everyone came to realize it would not be long before he would be gone.

While dad was at my uncle's house waiting to die, his female friend wasn't around as much. She would come by and visit, but I believe it was hard for her to see him in his deteriorating condition. Plus, with him being at my uncle's house, she was unable to have her "private time" with him as she would have liked.

I was a senior in high school and focused on graduating, all while praying dad would survive to make my graduation. Meanwhile, I still spent some weekends at home alone. When I wasn't at my uncle's house with immediate family caring for dad, my sister, his friend, and I would be at the apartment in Passaic, New Jersey. The last few months of running back and forth between the two homes soon took its toll on me.

Even though I had a license, I didn't drive without an adult in the car with me. Although no family member said it, I knew they did not trust me to drive by myself, especially after damaging my sister's car. I did not like having to wait on others and not being able to leave when I was ready to after spending time with dad. My brothers did not come by often to see dad due to family drama, specifically with my dad's female friend. Although it was not to the point of outright hatred, they could not tolerate one another's presence for long, which was not beneficial for my dad's wellbeing.

Dad's strength began to weaken, and, by the beginning of Spring in 1995, he was no longer moving around my uncle's house and was confined to his bed in my cousin's room. I don't recall the specifics of the weeks and days before his passing like I do the day he died. I remember finding out he was not doing well and may not last much longer.

That day, when I arrived, the family was very emotional. Everyone who needed to be there was, including my brother Don. However, my other brother was not. Dad was noticeably struggling to breathe and speak. The longer I was there, the more it became evident that he was not going to live much longer.

After being there for a while and absorbing everyone going through their emotions while coming to grips with the fact that dad would soon die, I decided to go back into the room with him once my brother, sister, and another family left. I stood afar off and looked at my dad. I became very emotional, walked out of the room, and stood in the hallway of my uncle's apartment. I remember my aunt seeing me leave the room emotional and tearing up, so she followed me down the hall and outside. I didn't have much to say to her, as I just wanted to be alone. She tried to console me, but eventually left and went back inside. I paced the hallway as an abundance of thoughts flowed through my mind. I remember thinking, "This is it. Dad is going to die. He will miss my graduation and everything else in my life." I cried uncontrollably and was confused, sad, hurt, and lonely. Whatever other negative or unhappy emotions you can think of, I both lived and felt them.

Just when the tears began to subside and I could breathe normally again, I heard a great scream and wailing. Someone yelled, "That's it! He is gone! Don is dying!" I ran down the hall, burst through the door, and ran straight to my dad's room. A few family members were standing outside of the room, with my brother being the only one at my dad's side. As he stood over my dad, he was emotional and crying. I approached and touched my dad on his leg while my brother held his hands. At the same moment I touched his leg, I watched as he took his last breath. My brother pleaded for him to arise and not be gone. As for me, I simply froze in place for a few moments and then walked out of the room, paced around the home for a bit, and then went back into the hallway and wept.

When I finally went back inside, everyone was in hysterics. It was pure mayhem. It was as if I was the only one who had not totally lost it emotionally. My sister was screaming like a demon, crying and hitting the bed, pillows, and any other soft thing she knew she wouldn't break. I stood alone for at least ten minutes before one of my cousins and aunt came over to attempt to comfort and console me.

I peeked into the room a few times after it was clear dad had died. I was numb and didn't know what was next. After all, I had never observed someone die and never watched a person go through sickness or disease that would eventually kill them.

Dad died on April 22, 1995, in his bed in my cousin's room at my aunt and uncle's home in East Orange, New Jersey. Dad left in his will that he wanted to be cremated, which he was. My sister still has possession of his urn to this day.

The ashes of Don Gabriel Pullen are encapsulated in an urn, but the soul, music, and legacy of Don Gabriel Pullen is still alive and well. From, his music and artwork being at the Smithsonian Institute, Library of Congress, and NPR radio in DC., too popular jazz magazines, and music databases in and out of the U.S., Down Beat magazine, and a Switzerland jazz Database Company. There is also a street in Georgia named after Pullen, and days dedicated to him and his music in Canada and Europe. Don Pullen has left a musical legacy for the world

I thank God I was and will always be a part of his legacy.

About the Author

KEITH G. PULLEN is "The Son of a Legend".

I am blessed, grateful, and excited about this book, and the opportunities it will present for others and myself. I have always enjoyed writing and expressing myself via writing. This book is my truth, experiences, and heart concerning my dad, his life, music, and what life was like for me growing up with my dad. My dad's music career and lifestyle enabled me to go to college and be in a position to learn life and educational skills to be able to provide for my daughter and myself.

Family is and always has been important to me, and I would not be who I am, and have this opportunity to publish a book, if it were not for family. Although, my dads' type of jazz was not very commercial, and many fans of jazz have never heard of my dad. His music impacted and change the genre of jazz, like no other musical talent form the Star City of Roanoke Va. I moved back to Roanoke, VA in 2006. The memories and moments I experienced in Roanoke as a child with family were very influential in the writing of this book. Sharing and exposing moments and stories about my experiences with my dad and family as a youth in Roanoke, is a crucial aspect of this book. I have a complex personality, and can be perceived as very opinionated and controversial, as my dad was. However, like my dad I am very committed to who and what I believe, believe in and love. As, a Christian – sharing and spreading Gods love to and for others, in and through my sins is important and necessary to and for my success in life. I believe that God inspired and lead me to write this book, and without faith to overcome, doubt, negative memories, pain, hurt, unforgiveness, and literally watching my dad die. I would not have been able to write and complete this book. My prayer and belief are that this book, will positively impact people specifically men, who may have experienced a lack of their father in their life on a consistent basis. The entire experience of writing and publishing a book, has been emotional, and life changing to and for me. I am excited about the journey future, and the possibility publishing more books about my life experiences, journey, God, and my relationship with God.

"I am Keith G. Pullen, and I am the son of a legend"

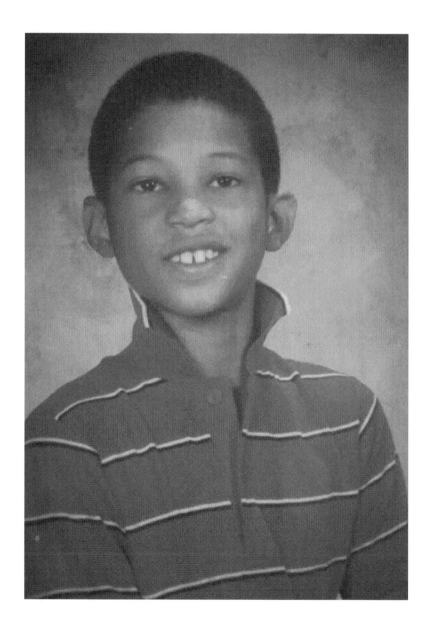

Made in the USA
Columbia, SC
21 November 2021